DISCARDED

Relaxation and Yoga

JOHN SON

Children's Press®
An Imprint of Scholastic Inc.

Content Consultant

Phyllis Meadows, PhD, MSN, RN
Associate Dean for Practice, Clinical Professor, Health Management and Policy
University of Michigan, Ann Arbor, Michigan

Library of Congress Cataloging-in-Publication Data
Names: Son, John, author.
Title: Relaxation and yoga / by John Son.
Other titles: True book.
Description: New York, NY : Children's Press, an imprint of Scholastic Inc.,
    2017. | Series: A true book
Identifiers: LCCN 2016013909| ISBN 9780531228470 (library binding) | ISBN
    9780531233290 (pbk.)
Subjects: LCSH: Hatha yoga—Juvenile literature. | Relaxation—Juvenile
    literature. | Health—Juvenile literature.
Classification: LCC RA781.7 .S6435 2017 | DDC 613.7/046—dc23
LC record available at https://lccn.loc.gov/2016013909

No part of this publication may be reproduced in whole or in part, or stored in a retrieval system, or transmitted in any form or by any means, electronic, mechanical, photocopying, recording, or otherwise, without written permission of the publisher. For information regarding permission, write to Scholastic Inc., Attention: Permissions Department, 557 Broadway, New York, NY 10012.

© 2017 Scholastic Inc.

All rights reserved. Published in 2017 by Children's Press, an imprint of Scholastic Inc.
Printed in China 62
SCHOLASTIC, CHILDREN'S PRESS, A TRUE BOOK™, and associated logos are trademarks and/or registered trademarks of Scholastic Inc.
1 2 3 4 5 6 7 8 9 10 R 26 25 24 23 22 21 20 19 18 17

Front cover: A woman meditating
Back cover: Students meditating in classroom

Find the Truth!

Everything you are about to read is true *except* for one of the sentences on this page.

Which one is **TRUE**?

T or F   Yoga is a competitive sport.

T or F   The goal of yoga is to feel comfortable with yourself.

Find the answers in this book.

Contents

Downward-facing
dog pose

Yoga equipment

THE **BIG** TRUTH!

The Big Truth!

Frog pose

You can practice yoga and relaxation techniques with your family.

The first known book on yoga was *The Yoga Sutras*, written roughly two thousand years ago.

CHAPTER 1

A Journey Into Our Bodies

Imagine you are sitting under a tree. The grass is soft and cool. A gentle breeze floats across your skin. Sunbeams flicker through the branches as Earth turns in space. Birds sing, a leaf flutters down, a butterfly lands on your knee. Everything is in its place. You are smiling and surrounded by wide-open spaces. What you imagine is calm and connected. This is exactly how you feel inside your body through the practice of yoga and relaxation. **Namaste**.

What Is Yoga?

Yoga means "to connect" or "bring together" in Sanskrit, an ancient language of India. In yoga, a person is considered to have three parts: body, mind, and heart. The body includes bones, muscles, organs, blood, and breath. The mind is one's thoughts, memories, and dreams. The heart is all a person feels, whether it's joy, sadness, anger, peace, or silliness. Yoga practice works to bring these parts together.

Sanskrit developed into Hindi, Bengali, and other modern languages used in and around India.

Yoga requires mental concentration as well as physical effort.

With practice, you can learn to become more comfortable, even in very stressful situations!

Find Your Seat

The goal of yoga practice is not to **compete**, but to sit comfortably. This doesn't always mean you are actually sitting. You can be standing, kneeling, speaking in front of a class, or visiting a new place. But you feel as comfortable as you do when you are sitting in your favorite spot. Yoga students stretch, stand, squat, and twist. Why? The more you move in your body, mind, and heart, the more you learn about yourself.

The work you do for the community when you volunteer can be considered an asana.

Asana

Asana means "seat" in Sanskrit. For yoga students, an asana is a **posture** or action that helps them find their seat. An asana can involve a student's body, thoughts, or actions. Or it can involve all three at once. Arching your back like a cat is an asana. Saying a kind word or helping someone in need is an asana. Eating healthy and taking your time walking, eating, or completing your chores are asanas, too.

Green Yoga

Yogis see all people as connected to one another and to the planet. As yoga students take care of themselves, they may extend that care to people around them. This includes family, friends, and classmates, as well as these people's families, people those families know, and so on. Caring for Earth and the people on it are, therefore, part of yoga practice. Examples include recycling and writing to a grandparent. Can you think of more?

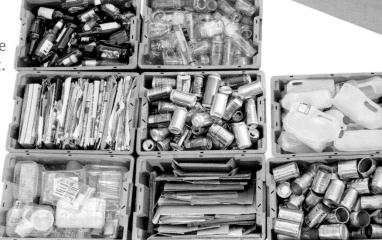

Recycling is one part of caring for the environment.

CHAPTER 2

Let's Do Yoga!

Your breath is like a thread that connects the different parts of you. When you breathe calmly through your nose, you can follow the rhythm of your breath. In this way, you can keep everything—body, mind, and heart—connected, even when you feel challenged or overwhelmed. So breathe in (inhale) and breathe out (exhale) as you practice a few basic yoga **poses**.

The number of U.S. adults practicing yoga grew from 4 million to more than 36 million between 2001 and 2016.

Cat and Cow Poses

Cat pose and cow pose can loosen you up if you feel stiff or tired.

1. Begin on your hands and knees. Your wrists are directly under your shoulders, and your knees are under your hips. Your feet are in line with your knees. Spread your fingers wide. Relax your neck and face.

2. Move into cow pose. Inhale through your nose. Let your belly sink toward the ground. Lift your chin and chest, and look up.

For cow pose, all you need is flat ground. Use a thin mat if your knees are uncomfortable.

3. Exhale through your nose and move into cat pose. Draw your belly in and round your back toward the sky, like a cat arching its back. Let the top of your head point toward the ground.

4. Inhale and move back into cow pose, then exhale into cat pose. As you do so, notice how your body feels. Repeat 5 to 10 times. Sit back on your heels when you are done.

Arch your back like a cat in cat pose.

Downward-facing dog pose reminds you that there is always another way of looking at things.

Downward-Facing Dog Pose

This pose strengthens your arms and legs and improves your **flexibility**.

1. Start on all fours, just as in cat and cow pose.
2. Press your palms into the floor. Lift your seat and straighten your legs to make an upside-down V. Release your heels to the floor.
3. Relax your head and neck down. Stay there for 5 to 10 calm breaths.
4. Lower your knees to the floor and sit back on your heels.

Bird Pose

It is important to not take yourself too seriously. Laugh when you fall and especially when you learn to fly!

1. Begin in mountain pose. To do this, stand tall with your feet together, knees relaxed, and arms by your side.

2. Inhale and reach your arms out to the side, like a T. Continue breathing.

3. Lean forward from your hips as you lift one leg straight behind you. Continue breathing, then return to mountain pose. Repeat on the other leg.

Bird pose improves your balance. It also strengthens your back and legs.

Frog Pose

The frog pose strengthens your legs, improves your flexibility, and develops your patience.

1. From mountain pose, separate your feet as wide as your shoulders. Sink into a squat position. Your hips should go below your knees, but your seat does not touch the ground.

2. Press your palms together in front of your chest. Press your elbows into your knees. Sit tall. Breathe through your nose.

3. Lower your seat to the floor to finish.

Stay in frog pose as long as you are comfortable.

Balance on your seat
in boat pose.

Boat Pose

Boat pose uses your whole body at once.

1. Sit on the ground. Bend your knees up so your feet are flat on the ground. Sit tall and relax your shoulders. Take a moment to breathe.

2. Lift your feet, keeping your knees bent. Reach your arms straight in front of you. Balance on your seat. Straighten your back. Breathe through your nose for up to 5 breaths.

3. When you are ready, return to your starting position.

Many different
people take part
in yoga today.

CHAPTER 3

What Yoga Can Give You

People have practiced yoga for thousands of years. It developed in India as early as 500 BCE. The teacher Swami Vivekananda first brought yoga ideas to Western countries in 1890. Today, yoga is practiced all over the world. It has had a positive impact on countless people, helping them learn to be calm and centered. Yoga is also good exercise. Students gain both strength and flexibility.

Thank your teacher before and after class by smiling and saying "Namaste."

Sometimes you may just need a break from your usual activities to daydream.

The Three Rs

Regular yoga practice helps improve your ability to listen to your body, thoughts, and feelings. This helps you know when to rest. Sometimes that means going to bed early or just turning off the computer and gazing out the window. Once you feel rested, you relax. You become calmer, clearer, and restored. You can then more effectively face whatever comes next. Rest, relax, restore—these are the three Rs.

Head and Shoulders, Knees and Toes

Yoga reminds us that we never stop learning about our bodies. We bend, stretch, and twist in our yoga poses. As we do so, we become more familiar with how all the bones, muscles, and joints work together. A strong relationship with our bodies helps us be positive about ourselves. It helps us feel good about ourselves and be proud of the unique way each of us appears in the world.

With time, yoga can help you build flexibility, strength, and coordination.

23

Inside Out

As you become more sensitive to your body through yoga, you also become more familiar with the way you feel inside. Yoga can help you develop a relationship with your feelings such as joy, anger, boredom, jealousy, excitement, loneliness, hurt, and pride. All of your feelings deserve your attention. The feelings of other people are also important.

It's all right to feel sad or lonely. These emotions are just as important and valid as happiness or excitement.

Practicing the three Rs can help you have an easier time paying attention in school.

In Focus

Sometimes it is difficult to sit down and do your homework or focus on what your teacher says. But if you are rested, relaxed, and restored, then attention and focus can come more easily. Studies have shown that yoga can help people who suffer from ADHD, or attention deficit/hyperactivity disorder. ADHD makes it difficult to focus or sit still for very long. Over time, consistent yoga practice helps improve the ability of those with ADHD to concentrate and stay calm.

Playtime

Do you enjoy riding a bicycle? Do you like knowing how to fix it when something goes wrong? For some people, figuring out how a bicycle works and how to take care of it helps them enjoy that bicycle even more! In a similar way, yoga and relaxation can help

you better enjoy being yourself. With practice, you can start to feel more enthusiastic and have a good time no matter what you are doing.

The better you understand your body, the more you can teach it to do!

Hugs From Amma

Since she was a young girl in southern India, Mata Amritanandamayi has helped those in need. One way she helps is by simply hugging people who seem to be sad or suffering. Because of her caring nature, people began to call her Amma, which means "mother." For more than three decades, Amma has traveled the world and hugged millions of people. It is her special way of practicing yoga.

Sometimes stressful
events can make
it feel almost
impossible to relax.

CHAPTER 4

Let's Relax!

Everyone experiences stress, worry, and anxiety. Our schedules can feel packed with homework and lessons and after-school activities. We may feel pressured to get better grades, compete harder, never make mistakes, and behave. People around us can be negative. Maybe we have trouble sleeping. The following yoga practices can help us rise above these times.

 About 18 percent of adults in the United States suffer from an anxiety disorder.

When you feel pressured or rushed, it's important to stop and take a breath.

Just Let Go

Sometimes, the world can feel difficult, crowded, or busy. At these times, you can try to find space, quiet, and calm inside you through **meditation**.

1. Find a place where you can be still (but not stiff) for a while. Sit comfortably with your back tall but not too straight. You may be on the floor kneeling, or sitting with your legs crossed or straight in front of you. You can also sit on a chair or against a wall.

2. Rest your hands on your thighs, palms facing up or down. Close your eyes and just breathe for a few minutes.

3. Bring your attention to your toes. Are they tense? Try to relax them. Move to your knees and do the same for them. Continue up the body, clear to the top of your head. Where are you tense? Ask yourself to relax.

4. Open your eyes. How do you feel?

Take your time when you meditate.

Back-to-Back Breathing

You can practice this method of breathing anywhere. You just need a partner.

1. Sit tall, back-to-back with your partner. Rest your legs in a comfortable position.

2. Place one hand over your heart and the other on your belly. Close your eyes. Breathe through your nose.

3. Notice your partner's breath. Is it fast? Slow? Can you breathe in time with your partner?

Timeline of the Growth of Yoga

500 BCE
The practice and philosophy of yoga begins to develop in India.

2nd century CE
The first of *The Yoga Sutras* by Patanjali are written.

Candle Pose

Spend a few minutes in this pose, especially if you can't fall asleep.

1. Lie flat on your back and breathe through your nose.

2. Slowly lift your legs straight up like a candle, making an L shape with your body. (You can also rest your legs against a wall.) Spread your arms out at a comfortable angle. Open your palms up toward the sky.

3. Close your eyes, relax your neck and face, and breathe.

1890

Swami Vivekananda tours the United States introducing yoga to the West.

2016

More than 36 million people practice a form of yoga and relaxation in the United States.

Yoga and Relaxation in School

A growing number of American schools offer forms of yoga and relaxation as an alternative to gym classes, recess, and break-time periods. Studies have shown that students who participate improve their test scores, have better focus, are calmer, and get along better with their classmates.

In some programs, students practice poses related to animals or objects in books they are reading. If a cat is featured in a book, for example, the students study the cat pose. A program director in Georgia explains, "It helps the kids feel like they're not [just] listening. It's interactive."

The director of a similar program in Maryland says that, for his students, "there is a lot more love for themselves and others."

Some parents object to yoga being taught in schools because they believe it is a religious practice. In a court case in San Diego, California, a judge ruled that yoga was not necessarily religious. As a result, it could be part of school activities. For now, the future of yoga and relaxation in schools looks bright.

A woman
practices yoga
in a park in
Spain.

CHAPTER 5

Who, Where, How

Today, millions of people practice some form of yoga and relaxation all over the world. You can find yoga studios in every major city across the United States. People of all ages, shapes, sizes, and abilities have made yoga a regular part of their lives. Despite its popularity, many people have yet to learn that you can practice yoga and relaxation anywhere, anytime.

 Breath control is referred to as *pranayama* in yoga.

Everybody Yoga!

Unlike some physical activities, yoga fits all sizes and levels of fitness. It is not the purpose of yoga to make everyone look, act, and feel the same. Instead, those who teach yoga strive to encourage students to feel at home with and safe as themselves. Students are only required to be willing to journey into their body.

A student stretches in yoga class with the help of her teacher.

Yoga Guru

Traditionally, yoga students stay close to a teacher, or **guru**. Gurus share their experience and provide hands-on guidance to help students practice safely and at a healthy pace. A teacher you feel comfortable with and who inspires you can help you get more out of your practice. If you live in a place where it's not easy to find a teacher, you can always connect to one offering classes online.

Your guru can help you grow in your yoga practice over time.

You can take your yoga practice with you wherever you go.

Here, There, and Everywhere

There are no limits to where you can practice yoga and relaxation. In some cities, classes have 100 students or more. You can also practice alone in your home. You can practice outdoors at the beach, in a park, or in your backyard. Some yoga poses are great for when you are sitting at your desk. You can even practice in a waiting room.

What You Need

All you need to practice yoga and relaxation is a little space, a flat surface, and comfortable clothes you can move around in. It is nice to have a yoga mat on which to practice. You may want to have a cushion or block to sit on during relaxation exercises as well. However, these objects are not necessary.

Using yoga mats, blocks, and straps to help stretch are common tools in yoga.

When you practice, you might enjoy having calm music in the background. Let your body take its time. If you force it to move into a position or at a speed it's not ready for, you can injure yourself. It is also best to avoid eating at least an hour before you practice.

Be sure to drink plenty of water or another healthy drink before and after you practice.

Namaste. ★

It's important to stay hydrated!

Bringing Yoga to the World

Bellur Krishnamachar Sundararaja (B. K. S.) Iyengar struggled with constant illness and pain as a child. When in his teens, Iyengar began learning yoga. Progress was difficult. But in time, Iyengar flourished. He began experimenting with ways to make yoga's asanas more accessible. His methods included props such as blocks, ropes, and blankets. These helped people enter poses and develop their abilities safely and comfortably. Iyengar's teachings changed yoga and won him followers around the world.

Number of U.S. adults who practiced a form of yoga and relaxation in 2016: More than 36 million

Percent of Americans practicing yoga who are male in 2016: 28

Percent of Americans practicing yoga who are female in 2016: 72

Number of U.S. children who practice a form of yoga and relaxation in 2012: 1.9 million

How much Americans spend a year on yoga classes and products: $10.3 billion, as of 2012

Did you find the truth?

F Yoga is a competitive sport.

T The goal of yoga is to feel comfortable with yourself.

Resources

Books

Harper, Jennifer Cohen. *Little Flower Yoga for Kids: A Yoga and Mindfulness Program to Help Your Child Improve Attention and Emotional Balance*. Oakland, CA: New Harbinger Publications, 2013.

Nhat Hanh, Thich. *A Handful of Quiet: Happiness in Four Pebbles*. Berkeley, CA: Plum Blossom Books, 2012.

Verde, Susan. *I Am Yoga*. New York: Abrams Books for Young Readers, 2015.

Visit this Scholastic Web site for more information on relaxation and yoga:
★ www.factsfornow.scholastic.com
Enter the keywords **Relaxation and Yoga**

Important Words

compete (kuhm-PEET) to try hard to outdo others at a task, race, or contest

flexibility (flek-suh-BIL-uh-tee) the ability to bend

guru (GOO-roo) a person who has special knowledge and who is looked up to by many people

meditation (med-uh-TAY-shuhn) thinking deeply and quietly

namaste (NAH-muh-stay) a greeting used across India and often at the beginning and end of yoga classes around the world

poses (POHZ-iz) particular positions that a person remains in for a certain amount of time

posture (PAHS-chur) the position of a person's body

yogis (YOH-geez) people who practice yoga

Index

Page numbers in **bold** indicate illustrations.

About the Author

John Son works in book publishing and teaches yoga in Brooklyn, New York. He loves watching students come into class tired and overwhelmed and leave smiling, glowing, and open. It works every time. His favorite student is his son, Theo. John is also the author of *Finding My Hat*, a book about his adventures growing up in Texas as a Korean American.

PHOTOGRAPHS ©: cover: Stockbyte/Thinkstock; back cover: skynesher/iStockphoto; 3: Jonathan Ross/Dreamstime; 4: Hangon Media Works Private limited/Alamy Images; 5 top: Khrystsina Tsarova/Dreamstime; 5 bottom: nanka/Shutterstock, Inc.; 6: Illya_Vinogradov/iStockphoto; 8: fizkes/Fotolia; 9: Christopher Robbins/Media Bakery; 10: Ariel Skelley/Media Bakery; 11: Dave and Les Jacobs/Media Bakery; 12: Dougal Waters/Media Bakery; 14: fizkes/Fotolia; 15: Ableimages/Superstock, Inc.; 16: Hangon Media Works Private limited/Alamy Images; 17: Charles C. Place/Getty Images; 18: nanka/Shutterstock, Inc.; 19: Rob Marmion/Shutterstock, Inc.; 20: Ariel Skelley/Media Bakery; 22: Darren Baker/Shutterstock, Inc.; 23: exopixel/Shutterstock, Inc.; 24: Stockbyte/Thinkstock; 25: Hill Street Studios/Media Bakery; 26: fizkes/Thinkstock; 27: Aijaz Rahi/AP Images; 28: Dennis Welsh/Media Bakery; 30: Mariasats/Dreamstime; 31: Jonathan Ross/Dreamstime; 32: World History Archive/Alamy Images; 33 left: Pictures From History/The Image Works; 33 right: Anna Furman/Shutterstock, Inc.; 34-35 background: P. Chinnapong/Shutterstock, Inc.; 34 main: Amelie-Benoist/BSIP/Superstock, Inc.; 35 top: The Star-Ledger/Mitsu Yasukawa/The Image Works; 35 bottom: skynesher/iStockphoto; 36: Ben Welsh/Design Pics/Superstock, Inc.; 38: Jetta Productions/Walter Hodges/Media Bakery; 39: ElNariz/Thinkstock; 40: Blend Images/Alamy Images; 41: Khrystsina Tsarova/Dreamstime; 42: Louis-Paul St-Onge/Thinkstock; 43: Dinodia/age fotostock; 44: Dougal Waters/Media Bakery.